Europe's New Defense Ambitions: Implications for NATO, the US, and Russia

By Peter van Ham

Dr. Peter van Ham is a professor of West European Politics at the George C. Marshall European Center for Security Studies, Garmisch–Partenkirchen, Germany. He recently published *A Critical Approach to European Security* (London: Pinter, 1999). A new book on European integration theory (*European Integration and the Postmodern Condition*) is forthcoming from Routledge (2001).

Foreword

The George C. Marshall European Center for Security Studies is proud to issue this inaugural edition of the *Marshall Center Papers*. Dr. Peter van Ham's paper, "Europe's New Defense Ambitions: Implications for NATO, the US, and Russia," sets the tone for our new monograph series. The *Marshall Center Papers* are specifically created to disseminate scholarly monographs that explore and influence the resolution of Atlantic-European-Eurasian security issues. Dr. van Ham's paper provides an articulate analysis of the most vital of current international defense issues: the future of cooperative security in Europe.

The search for a European security identity periodically opens major debates that push policy makers in new, sometimes revolutionary directions. The war in Kosovo and the American-dominated air campaign have rekindled an old debate on the future of European defense capabilities. At issue is how to resolve the potential contradictions between a "Common European Security and Defense Policy" and the maintenance of a strong transatlantic alliance.

At the same time, the European Union has set itself the remarkable task of rapidly absorbing the Western European Union and creating a European rapid reaction corps. Both the speed and the scope of these reforms are impressive. They may alter the strategic landscape quite fundamentally. The United States has officially endorsed the European goals, although warning against the three "D"s— Duplication, Decoupling, and Discrimination.

Peter van Ham has devoted this study to exploring the impact of the Common European Security and Defense Policy upon NATO, the United States, and Russia. He laments the lack of frankness in recent debates and poses a number of sensitive questions. Will Russia turn hostile to European ambitions, as the European Union acquires military muscle? Will the United States have to accept the duplication of some NATO assets? Will the Central Europeans first suffer from discrimination (because few of them will soon join the European Union) and then worry about the decoupling of the Atlantic Alliance? His answers are provocative but scholarly, and his prediction of growing tensions in the Atlantic Alliance deserves a wide readership.

Robert Kennedy, PhD
Director
George C. Marshall European Center for Security Studies

Executive Summary

At the European Union's Helsinki summit of December 1999, European leaders took a decisive step toward the development of a new Common European Security and Defense Policy (CESDP) aimed at giving the European Union (EU) a stronger role in international affairs backed by a credible military force. At Helsinki, EU Member States committed themselves to a number of military "headline goals": by the year 2003, the EU should be able to deploy up to 60,000 troops for so–called "Petersberg" (i.e., humanitarian, rescue, and peacekeeping) missions. This new EU–led rapid reaction force should be deployable within 60 days and be able to sustain deployment for at least one year.

This *Marshall Center Paper* analyzes the processes leading to Helsinki by examining why and how this new European consensus on defense issues came about. It takes the pulse of the EU's emerging defense policy and touches upon the main controversies and challenges that still lie ahead. What are the national interests and driving forces behind it, and what steps still need to be taken to realize Europe's ambitions to achieve a workable European crisis management capability? Particular attention is paid to the implications of an emerging European defense capability for the future of the North Atlantic Treaty Organization (NATO), the transatlantic relationship, and the role of Russia in Europe.

The paper argues that the political and strategic consequences of injecting defense issues into the structures of the EU remain unclear. Although Europe's defense ambitions are not designed to undermine NATO, they do place into question NATO's future role in the management of European security. Transatlantic tensions over the relationship between the "New EU" (i.e., an EU with its own military capabilities) and NATO are already evident. The Kosovo air war of Spring 1999 was a turning point for Europeans, in that the war highlighted the superiority of American military resources and infrastructures. The war demonstrated that, despite years of talk and paperwork, Europeans were still unable to back up their economic and diplomatic prowess with military means. "Kosovo" made it painfully clear that Europe depends upon American military capabilities. It also accentuated the fact that US leadership in Europe is problematic and that Washington is unwilling to incur casualties in European conflicts where US national interests are not clearly at stake.

The paper looks at three policy issues that remain unresolved and that are bound to cause transatlantic problems over the next few years. The first is how closely should the EU's CESDP duplicate NATO's existing capabilities and institutional structures? The second concerns how to "sequence" the decision making processes in case of wars or crises and in the real military challenges the EU is likely to face in the decade ahead. The third involves the impact of a new strategic balance within the Atlantic Alliance on Europe's defense industrial base, and *vice versa*.

However, the EU's recent foray into things military has wider implications. For example, how will Moscow come to see the prospective enlargement of the EU in the direction of Central Europe—possibly including the Baltic states—when such an expansion would extend Europe's "sphere of influence" toward the territory of the former Soviet Union? Will Russia alter its now rather positive attitude toward EU enlargement and adopt a more hostile approach when the EU takes on a more military guise? The general trend in governmental circles in Moscow is to welcome the EU's military plans as a step to rid Europe of American hegemony and NATO–centrism. From this perspective, a European CESDP is looked upon as a means to preclude a unipolar world led by the United States.

Not very surprisingly, this may also be one of the main reasons why many Central European countries are cautious about dealing with defense issues outside the well–known and tested NATO framework. Countries like the Czech Republic, Hungary, and Poland fear that Europe's defense plans may undermine the relevance of NATO. The EU's new defense ambitions are also of concern to western allies outside the EU who are anxious to keep NATO as the ultimate center for the organization of European security. Although neither Russia nor Central Europe is part of the EU, their worries and concerns are going to have an impact on how Europe's defense plans develop. Although Russia's reactions to the EU's new defense ambitions remain ambivalent, it is unlikely that its position will pose serious difficulties for the EU's overall strategy to integrate Russia into Europe.

The paper concludes that the EU's new defense moves illustrate that EU Member States now consider the risk that a new European military force might undermine NATO is less significant than the threat posed by the *status quo*. Without a rebalanced transatlantic relationship, NATO would certainly fall into decay. However, if Europe's CESDP is injudiciously managed, Europe may end up with the worst of both worlds: a weak EU and a weakened NATO. ∎

Europe's New Defense Ambitions: Implications for NATO, the US, and Russia

Introduction[1]

At the European Union's Helsinki summit on December 10–11, 1999, European leaders took a decisive step toward the development of a new Common European Security and Defense Policy (CESDP) aimed at giving the European Union (EU) a stronger role in international affairs backed by credible military force. After many years of talking about a possible European Common Defense Policy (CDP), European governments finally defined the military dimension of their economic and political union. This remarkable expression of collective political will to build a European defense capability is a defining moment in the process of European integration, giving the EU for the first time since 1954—when the attempt to set up a European Defense Community (EDC) failed—a distinct military component.

This paper analyzes the processes that led to Helsinki by examining why and how this new European consensus on defense issues came about. What are the national interests and driving forces behind it, and what steps still need to be taken to realize Europe's ambitions to achieve a workable European crisis management capability? Obviously a lot needs to be done to provide the EU with a powerful military force capable of acting autonomously in and around Europe. Particular attention will be paid to the implications of an emerging European defense capability for the futures of both the North Atlantic Treaty Organization (NATO) and the transatlantic relationship, as well as its impact on the role of Russia in Europe.

Although Europe's defense ambitions are not designed to undermine NATO, the EU's new plans do raise questions about the role NATO is to play in the management of European security in the decade to come. Transatlantic tensions over the relationship between the "New EU" (i.e., an EU with its own military capabilities) and NATO are already evident. NATO's Secretary General Lord Robertson captured this unease well, by arguing that "[t]here has always been a bit of schizophrenia about America, on the one hand saying 'You Europeans have got to carry more of the burden,' and then when the Europeans say 'OK, we'll carry more of the burden,' they say 'Well, wait a minute, are you trying to tell us to go home?'"[2] The transatlantic strain over the organization of European defense also testifies to significant differences in strategic vision, as well as in the practicalities of force planning and military capabilities. Whereas the United States has a global vision, the EU's emerging defense strategy and military planning will focus almost entirely on the European region. This global/regional dichotomy is bound to increase US–EU tensions over security strategy. This, in turn, may exacerbate American concern over Europe's latest defense ambitions.

What is more, given the process of European integration, a distinct military character will alter the EU's relationship with Russia. The EU has now initiated accession negotiations with the majority of Central European countries who want to join the European integration process primarily for economic and political reasons, and who still look to NATO as the principal source of their "hard" (i.e., military) security. But, how will Moscow come to see the prospective enlargement of the EU in the direction of Central Europe, possibly including the Baltic states, when such an expansion would extend Europe's "sphere of influence" toward the territory of the former Soviet Union? Perhaps Russia will alter its now rather positive attitude toward EU enlargement and adopt a more hostile approach when the EU takes on a more military guise? Europe's recent foray into things military is also of concern to western allies outside the EU who are anxious to keep NATO as the ultimate center for the organization of European security. Although neither Russia nor Central Europe is part of the EU, their worries and concerns are going to have an impact on the further development of Europe's new defense plans.

This *Marshall Center Paper* takes the pulse of the EU's emerging defense policy and touches upon the main controversies and challenges that still exist between good intentions and the creation of rapidly deployable expeditionary forces that would give Europe's diplomacy a military backbone. The paper will argue that the implications of injecting defense issues into the structures of the EU remain unclear and that the practical organization of the CESDP will pose a serious challenge to both Europe and the United States to maintain NATO's leading role in European security. Although Russia's reactions remain ambivalent to the EU's new defense ambitions, it is unlikely that its position will pose serious difficulties in the EU's overall strategy to integrate Russia into Europe.

The Road Toward a Common European Defense Policy

Two events have stimulated European governments to rethink their commitment to define a common European defense policy and capability. The first took place in 1997 when the Labour government of Prime Minister Tony Blair, determined to demonstrate the United Kingdom's central role in Europe, took the initiative on the restructuring of European defense cooperation. This was done in part to compensate for the United Kingdom's self–chosen exclusion from other

3

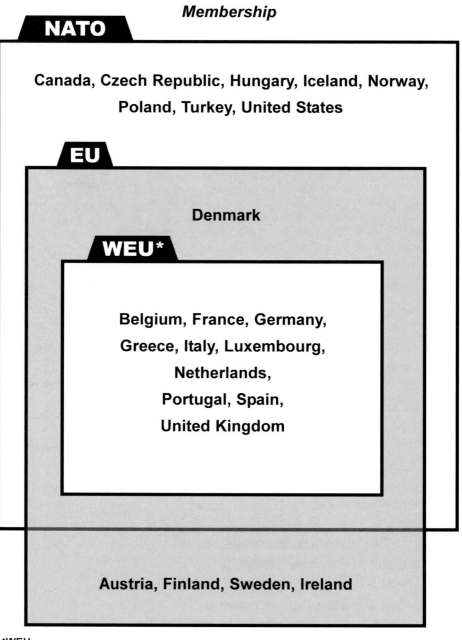

Membership

NATO

Canada, Czech Republic, Hungary, Iceland, Norway, Poland, Turkey, United States

EU

Denmark

WEU*

Belgium, France, Germany, Greece, Italy, Luxembourg, Netherlands, Portugal, Spain, United Kingdom

Austria, Finland, Sweden, Ireland

*WEU:
Associate Members: the Czech Republic, Hungary, Iceland, Norway, Poland, Turkey
Associate Partners: Bulgaria, Estonia, Latvia, Lithuania, Romania, Slovakia, and Slovenia
Observers: Denmark, Austria, Finland, Ireland, and Sweden

European projects—most notably the European Monetary Union (EMU).

The other turning point for the Europeans was the Kosovo air war. The war made it clear that the United States had better resources for intelligence, surveillance, and reconnaissance; more accurate precision–guided munitions; as well as superior air and sealift resources, logistics, and communications. The Kosovo experience highlighted, in dramatic relief, NATO's internal capability gap. It demonstrated that, despite years of talk and paperwork, Europeans could still not back up their economic and diplomatic prowess with military means. Most EU Member States—particularly France and the United Kingdom—were also deeply concerned about the complex and inept EU/Western European Union (WEU) and NATO decision making processes for European military crisis management. The Kosovo crisis has, therefore, done more for the development of Europe's defense identity than the decade of post–Maastricht deliberations on the EU's Common Foreign and Security Policy (CFSP) and its ensuing CDP.

At the informal European Council meeting in the Austrian town of Pörtschach, October 24–25, 1998, Britain for the first time publicly referred to its altered position on European defense cooperation, stating that Europe's Bosnia and Kosovo policies were "unacceptable" and marked by "weakness and confusion." Pörtschach, therefore, symbolizes the first, explicit step by EU Member States toward establishing a European crisis management capability backed by a more effective military infrastructure.

The European defense debate received additional momentum with the "Joint Declaration on European Defence," the joint *communiqué* generated by the Franco–British summit in St. Malo, France, on December 3–4, 1998. St. Malo was hailed by officials and the media alike as a true "watershed" in the EU's security approach. St. Malo was seen as opening the door to the possibility of a genuine Europeanization of defense in the decade to come. For the first time, Europe's defense ambitions dealt with military substance rather than with institutional niceties. St. Malo accepted the French position that the "Union must have the capability for autonomous action" on defense matters; whereas Britain was keen to stress the organic link between the EU and NATO. Both countries declared that "the Union must be given appropriate structures and a capacity for analysis of situation, sources of intelligence and a capability for relevant strategic planning, without unnecessary duplication" of what already exists within NATO.

Although much remained undefined at St. Malo (the EU's ties with WEU, for example), it is difficult to overstate the historic significance of the intensification of Franco–British security cooperation that took place. Without the combined political and military weight of both countries it would be impossible to envision a credible common European defense policy. Under Tony Blair, Downing Street adopted the French view that a more robust European defense capability would not undermine the transatlantic relationship, but would, quite to the contrary, be an essential element that would keep the Atlantic Alliance relevant and the United States involved in the management of European security. By crossing the European Rubicon on defense issues, Britain opened a new chapter in European integration, permitting a new security and defense dialogue

Britain opened a new chapter in European integration by crossing the European Rubicon on defense issues

between "Brussels" and Washington. Initially, Paris seemed to be both puzzled and irritated by the sudden change in Britain's position on European defense. French officials, therefore, accentuated the continued relevance of WEU and the necessity to keep European resources and decision making structures independent of NATO and the United States. France further argued for a strong EU–based military committee; for the EU to have the capacity for autonomous action without recourse to NATO assets; for the urgent development of European strategic transport and intelligence capabilities; and, as well, for the preservation of an Article V (collective defense) commitment among the full members of WEU.

Kosovo: A Watershed in European Defense. The combined German presidencies of the EU and WEU during the first half of 1999 gave Berlin an opportunity to develop the new impetus to give the CFSP credible operational capabilities and to prepare the ground for the required institutional changes in the EU's infrastructure. At the same time as the debate ensued concerning a new EU defense role, developments in Kosovo confronted European governments with the fact that they were militarily impotent to support regional crisis management, even in a situation that was in immediate geographic proximity.

The war over Kosovo quickly became a turning point. It was because of Kosovo that Europe was forced to reconsider what the EU/WEU and NATO could, and should, be able to do in the complex fields of crisis prevention, crisis management, peacekeeping, and warfare.[3] From the onset of the war, Washington determined the tone and policies of the "international community." During the war the United States quite literally called most of the shots, while the European allies played a more modest and low–key role. Although

7

NATO policy guided the war and was agreed upon in the North Atlantic Council (NAC), among no less than 19 countries, almost all of the intelligence information upon which decisions were made (i.e., where, when, and what to bomb) came from American sources. The missions were then mainly executed by American aircrews, mainly using the American military infrastructure.

> **Kosovo made it painfully clear that Europe depends upon American military capabilities, yet US leadership in Europe is tenuous**

"Kosovo" made it painfully clear that Europe depends upon American military capabilities. However, it also underlined the reality that US leadership in Europe is tenuous and that most Americans are unwilling to risk their lives in messy European conflicts in which their national interests are hardly at stake. The lesson for Europeans is evident: the United States remains crucial for the maintenance of the peace and security of the continent as long as Europe lacks the willingness to assume more responsibility for its own defense. This main "lesson of Kosovo" has, therefore, stimulated a rethinking of European defense cooperation, not in order to undermine NATO, but to provide the EU with the military means to support its available diplomatic means. No European country today calls for a European army, but most call for Europe to embrace the necessity of establishing a partnership with the United States based on more balanced military capabilities and shared political leadership. In March 1999, Prime Minister Blair noted that "[w]e Europeans should not expect the United States to have to play a part in every disorder in our own back yard. The European Union should be able to take on some security tasks on our own, and we will do better through a common European effort than we can by individual countries acting on their own."[4]

NATO's Washington summit on April 24, 1999, basically supported the trend toward a more pronounced and forceful European defense capability. The summit *communiqué* acknowledged "the resolve of the EU to have the capacity for autonomous action so that it can take decisions and approve military action where the Alliance as a whole is not engaged." It was stated that NATO was prepared to make "the necessary arrangements" to give the EU access to the collective assets and capabilities of the Alliance, as well as to ensure the EU access to NATO's planning capabilities. However, despite the rhetoric of transatlantic cooperation, considerable controversy remained after the summit over the exact meaning of "autonomous action," "ready access," and the "presumption of availability" of NATO assets.

At the EU's subsequent summit in Cologne, Germany, June 3–4, 1999, European governments committed themselves for the first time unequivocally to a common European defense policy. They declared that "the Union must have the capability for autonomous action, backed up by credible military forces, the means to decide to use them, and a readiness to do so, in order to respond to international crises without prejudice to actions by NATO." In order to achieve this goal, EU leaders saw the need to strengthen European capabilities in the fields of intelligence; strategic transport; command and control—which implies efforts to adapt, exercise, and bring together national and multinational European forces; as well as to strengthen the industrial and technological defense base. At Cologne, EU Member States also prepared the political ground to put into place the appropriate decision making mechanisms for crisis

EU leaders added military muscle to Europe's already significant economic and financial clout by establishing new permanent political and military bodies within the EU Council

management and to secure political control and strategic direction of future EU–led military operations.[5]

Modalities of Europe's Common Defense. The decisions reached at Cologne were formalized at the EU's Helsinki summit of December 1999. Many important questions were left unresolved, but decisions were made in Helsinki that allowed Europe's future defense structure to be formulated. EU leaders decided to add military muscle to Europe's already significant economic and financial clout by establishing new permanent political and military bodies within the EU Council:

• A standing Political and Security Committee (PSC), to deal with all aspects of the CFSP, including the CESDP. During a military crisis, this PSC will exercise political and strategic direction of the operation—under the authority of the Council;

• A Military Committee (MC), composed of EU Member States' Chiefs of Defense, or their military representatives. The MC will give military advice and make recommendations to the PSC; and

• A Military Staff (MS) to provide the Council with military expertise and support to the CESDP. The MS will perform early warning, situation assessment, and strategic planning for the EU's conflict prevention and crisis management ("Petersberg") tasks.

At Helsinki, EU Member States further committed themselves to a number of military "headline goals": by the year 2003, the EU should be able to deploy up to 15 brigades (or 50,000–60,000 troops) for Petersberg missions. The brigades should be militarily self–sustaining and be comprised of the necessary command, control, and intelligence capabilities; logistics; and other infrastructures, to include about 500 aircraft and 15 ships. These new EU troops should be rapidly deployable—within 60 days—and be able to sustain such a deployment for at least 1 year. Around 150,000 troops will be required for rotation purposes. The main aim would, therefore, be for EU states to have enough forces at hand to form the equivalent of an army corps of anywhere from 40,000 to 60,000 men. Such a corps would out of necessity be self–sufficient in terms of logistics, intelligence, and communications, and be ready for use in time of need for tasks in which the United States and/or NATO decide not to become engaged.

In order to prepare for these huge changes within the EU, the Union's General Affairs Council will work with the 15 EU national Defense Ministers to expand on the headline and capability goals. These EU Defense Ministers decided at an informal meeting in Sintra, Portugal, in February 2000, that the EU's temporary structures, the Political and Security Committee (PSC), Military Committee (MC), and Military Staff (MS), would prepare to start their operations in March 2000. A so–called Force Generation Conference is to be held at the end of 2000. At that conference each Member State will earmark the resources it can contribute to the EU's rapid reaction force. The EU also intends to increase its efforts to encourage the restructuring of the European defense industry to make sure that the CESDP will have a solid basis for

autonomous action and not be dependent upon external—
mostly US—military infrastructures and equipment. France
and the United Kingdom have made their joint service
headquarters available for commanding EU–led military
operations.[6]

Although the dimensions of the CESDP are now becoming
clear, much remains vague and undecided. It is, for example,
questionable that the EU can set up a credible and effective
military infrastructure without *de facto* setting up a "general
staff" and creating its own military chain–of–command. For
the time being, many EU Member States seem reluctant to go
that far, mainly because this would acknowledge the need for
further duplication of NATO functions. The Helsinki
declaration is also elusive on how working relations with
NATO should be developed over the months to come. Starting
with the statement that "[t]he European Union should have the
autonomous capacity to take decisions and, where NATO as a
whole is not engaged, to launch and then to conduct EU–led
military operations," it also affirms a willingness to conduct
"the necessary dialogue, consultation and cooperation with
NATO and its non–EU members." However, because this
should be done only "with full respect for the decision–making
autonomy of the EU and the single institutional framework of
the Union," it remains unclear what impact non–EU states can
have on Europe's CESDP. (See below for a more in–depth
debate of this issue.) The more exact and concrete modalities
for consultation, cooperation, and transparency between the
EU and NATO—and especially with the United States—are
still to be developed. In the meantime much will, therefore,
depend upon the informal contacts between the EU's High
Representative for CFSP, Javier Solana, and NATO's new
Secretary General, Lord Robertson.

Finding a New Transatlantic Military Balance

Ever since NATO's Brussels summit of 1994, the United States has, at least rhetorically, supported the development of a European Security and Defense Identity (ESDI) and expressed its readiness to make Alliance assets and capabilities available for WEU operations. Although American media were somewhat dumbfounded by what was generally seen as an overly ambitious European attempt to go it alone and establish a European military union (akin to the other EMU), US officials have aired their agreement with Europe's military push. At first, however, Washington was concerned with the message of the EU's Cologne summit of June 1999, where the Europeans proposed to give the EU a defense character without committing themselves concretely to a commensurate increase in Europe's military capabilities. In this respect, the subsequent Helsinki summit was reassuring to the United States, because it embedded the CESDP within the Atlantic security framework and followed through with concrete military headline goals.

In December 1999, following the Helsinki summit, US Deputy Secretary of State Strobe Talbott argued that "[t]here should be no confusion about America's position on the need for a stronger Europe. We are not against; we are not ambivalent; we are not anxious; we are for it. We want to see a Europe that can act effectively through the Alliance or, if NATO is not engaged, on its own. Period, end of debate."[7] But, of course, the transatlantic debate over the reorganization of European security and defense has just started in earnest, with many a serious quarrel and argument lying ahead. One of the main questions will be why, or perhaps even *whether*, the United States has given up its resistance to the organization of European defense within the EU. (Of course, answering this question depends to a large extent on the outcome of the US presidential elections of November 2000. An Al Gore administration may be more supportive of Europe's new defense ambitions than a George W. Bush administration.)

One classical American argument against an EU–based security system is that this would provide a backdoor security guarantee to EU members, both present and future, who are not covered by NATO's Article 5. Because EU Member States like Finland and Austria, who are not members of NATO, will participate fully in the EU's CESDP, they will indirectly affect the European input into NATO and may in crisis situations call upon the United States for military assistance. Other crucial questions remain outstanding: Are policy makers in Washington no longer concerned about the possible emergence of an "EU caucus" within NATO which may present the United States with inflexible European policy positions and *faits accomplis*? Is America now ready to give up its influence over European security and hand over its position of benign hegemonic leadership to the EU?

The Kosovo experience taught Europeans some embarrassing lessons and convinced many in the United States that crises in the EU's backyard should be solved by the Europeans themselves

Clearly, the British change of heart on European defense urges the United States to rethink its attitude toward the EU's budding defense ambitions. Now that Washington has "lost" its staunchest ally with an undiluted Atlanticist security orientation, the United States feels that the vitality of the Alliance may well be renewed by supporting the CESDP. What is more, the Kosovo experience not only offered Europeans some embarrassing lessons, but it convinced many in the United States that crises in the EU's backyard should preferably be solved by the Europeans themselves. However, the timing and the vague modalities of Europe's defense adolescence still trigger ample American *Angst*. Secretary of State Madeleine Albright's famous "three D"s illustrate these concerns. Washington does not want: a *decoupling* of Europe's security from that of America's; a *duplication* of effort and capabilities; or *discrimination* against those allies outside the EU. Although Lord Robertson formulated a looser, and less negative, "three I"s (i.e., the *indivisibility* of the transatlantic link; the *improvement* of European capabilities; and the *inclusiveness* of all allies in Europe's defense policy), working out the difficult practicalities of the CESDP is bound to become a source of strain in US–EU relations.

America's Ambiguous Enthusiasm. Apart from good intentions on both sides of the Atlantic, little is clear in the emerging new balance of power between the EU and NATO and, hence, between "Europe" and the United States. Whereas WEU has always been an unequal partner of NATO in the defense field, the EU is bound to play a much more assertive and forceful role in shaping Europe's institutional security landscape. Unlike NATO, the "New EU" will not only have a sturdy military capability at its disposal, but also a broad arsenal of economic, financial, and political instruments of statecraft. Given that most of Europe's regional problems and conflicts may not be truly resolved by military means—at least not in the long run—the EU is bound to become the actor of choice to address European security challenges.

To all but a few Atlanticist purists, it is obvious that the strategic balance within NATO is in need of urgent change.

Although the Kosovo experience has exposed this unhealthy imbalance within the Atlantic Alliance, the lack of frankness in the debate remains worrisome.[8] Europeans and Americans alike know that NATO and the transatlantic relationship have to be recast and that this will be a painful and problematic exercise. It seems fair to say that if the EU is serious about its intent to establish a common European defense policy, the ultimate objective is to lessen Europe's military dependency on America. Meanwhile, the EU now wants to have the possibility of fighting a Kosovo–like war without the consent and military support of the United States. This is, one would assume, nothing to be ashamed of and should be considered a normal ambition for an economic and political superpower–in–the–making like the EU. However, underneath the varnish of the Clinton administration's cautious support lingers the concern that a more self–reliant Europe will undermine the old NATO tradition of US hegemony and, therefore, risk a transatlantic decoupling. Both Europeans and Americans also fear that an increasingly isolationist and unilateralist US Congress might react to a stronger European defense by arguing that it is now time to leave European security to the EU and bring home American troops.[9] On the other hand, it is understood that the US Congress may well be more likely to continue its support for NATO if the Europeans are serious defense partners. Based on the EU's new defense moves, EU Member States have decided that the risk that a new European military force might undermine NATO is less significant than the threat posed by the *status quo*. Given these political imponderables, much attention is being paid to the managing and packaging of a rebalanced EU–US/NATO relationship.

There are three questions that remain unresolved that are bound to cause transatlantic problems over the next few years.

The first is how closely should the EU's CESDP duplicate NATO's existing capabilities and institutional structures? The second concerns how to "sequence" the decision making processes in case of wars or crises and in the real military challenges the EU is likely to face in the decade ahead. The third involves the impact of the new strategic balance within the Alliance on Europe's defense industrial base—and *vice versa*.

The Duplication Dilemma. French Defense Minister Alain Richard argued that "[w]hat fear of duplication really conceals is worry [in the United States] about the appearance of a new political partner, the European Union."[10] Although the Helsinki decisions look impressive on paper, it is clear that the EU's military infrastructure will remain rather modest and nowhere near the size of the NATO military staff. A European military secretariat, reporting to Solana, will decide how many military planners the EU needs in its defense organization. The EU's defense organization will, in any case, draw heavily on planning done in the EU's Member States. The EU's plans certainly do not involve, or imply, setting up standing European armed forces with a permanent multinational command, at least not for the near future. But, it will be difficult to foresee a serious CESDP that does not acquire better defense technology, better trained and deployable troops, as well as at least some parallel military structure.

It is on this point that Europe's harsh political reality could start to overtake the strategy laid out at Helsinki, because it seems evident that EU Member States at present do not wish to allocate sufficient money to buy first–class, home–grown defense systems—ranging from intelligence gathering equipment, precision–guided weapons, and electronic warfare capabilities, to search and rescue forces. Although Europe

NATO's European members had two million soldiers, yet had difficulty providing 40,000 troops for Kosovo spends 60 per cent of what the United States does on defense, the Kosovo war exposed Europe's weaknesses. Despite having two million people in uniform, NATO's European members were hardly able to place 40,000 troops in position in time to fight a regional war. Most European troops are still designed to repel a Soviet ground attack, rather than to rapidly deploy troops to nearby crisis situations. Because there is hardly any public support to increase defense spending, much is being made of trying to spend money more wisely and operating more efficiently by cooperating more closely on the European level. Lord Robertson argued perceptively that "[i]f you've got a budget that is 60 per cent of the American budget and is probably turning out 10 per cent of the capability then that is your first big problem . . . You can actually spend more money quite easily and get zero increase in capability."[11]

But, is it really realistic to assume that Europe is spending enough on defense and all it needs to do is create more synergy and achieve more efficient defense cooperation? Money may be better spent to get "more bang for the Euro," but, as John Chipman has argued: "Unless defense expenditure is allowed substantially to increase, the build–up of a serious [European] defense capacity will remain the stuff of *communiqués*."[12] According to NATO figures, the United States spends about 3.2 per cent of its GDP on defense (down from 6 per cent during the Cold War), with France and the United Kingdom spending 2.8 and 2.6 per cent, respectively; Germany (1.5) and Spain (1.4) find themselves at the low end of the spectrum. On average, defense spending by NATO's European members has dropped by 22 per cent since 1992. It is of no surprise, therefore, that the United States is calling upon its European allies to take on a bigger share of the defense burden within NATO. In December 1999, US Secretary of Defense William Cohen criticized Germany for spending too little on defense, arguing that this has a "profound and lasting impact on the capabilities, not only of [Germany], but of the alliance as a whole."[13]

It is in this context that EU Member States may well decide to set spending targets for buying new satellite–based navigation and guidance systems, fighter airplanes and transport aircraft, and the other defense equipment needed to make European forces deployable within the 60–day target. In the run up to Helsinki, several proposals were aired, ranging from clear–cut defense convergence criteria (by François Heisbourg), which would include a 2 per cent minimum of GDP for defense and a 30–40 per cent minimum of the defense budget for procurement and R&D, to suggestions for a so–called European System of Force Elements (by Tim Garden and John Roper) for financing, military planning, and command arrangements.[14] However, for those countries that still have to reach the Maastricht government debt criteria (which include Austria, France, Germany, the Netherlands, and Spain), it will be problematic to spend significantly more on defense without breaching EMU commitments. Politically, it will also be difficult to assure that no EU Member State drags its feet on defense spending in order to take a free ride on Europe's CESDP. A Europe based on political solidarity can not accept the silent NATO rule "who pays, plays." However, even if the Europeans were willing to spend more on defense and set up defense benchmarks, the political momentum of the EU's CESDP implies that they will "buy European." This will receive a very cool reception in Washington and is likely to increase tensions within the Alliance.

Although the EU's Helsinki *communiqué* stresses the need to avoid "unnecessary duplication" of the EU's defense organization with that of NATO, it is clear that some duplication of capabilities and infrastructure is inevitable and, probably, even beneficial. It should not be overlooked that most of WEU already duplicates, in one way or another, NATO structures. The EU has, therefore, accepted that *some* duplication of effort and organization is foreseeable. If Europe's new defense ambitions were to provide Europeans with more military capabilities (i.e., more strategic transport and intelligence capabilities), thereby duplicating what the United States already has available, this would be the type of replication all NATO allies could happily live with.

NATO's Fading Centrality. Another issue which will have to be thrashed out is the future relationship between the "New EU" and NATO. Non–EU NATO members have made it clear that they want to be involved in the decision shaping process on European defense. The United States has tried to formalize the EU–NATO relationship on these issues, but France has blocked these efforts and claims that the Europeans first have to clarify their military ambitions among themselves. Paris also argues that, for the time being, WEU should be the institution of choice for debating defense issues with other European countries, as well as with Turkey and the United States. The EU has, however, decided to embark upon strengthening ties between the European Parliament (to include its working groups and committees) and NATO's North Atlantic Assembly.

Another part of this debate is the vital question of whether NATO has to be consulted first, before any independent European military action will be undertaken. In the lead up to the Helsinki summit, Washington made it clear that before the

EU decides to act on its own in a crisis situation—with or without the use of NATO assets—NATO should be given a first option, or a right of first refusal, to intervene. This problem of the order in which decisions are to be made, in short "sequencing," is important, because at NATO's Washington summit in April 1999 it was agreed that the EU would have a "presumed access" to Alliance assets should US troops not become involved in a specific military operation. American officials also made it clear that "[e]ven if Washington decides not to send troops, we still want to be involved in the decision–making process from the beginning."[15]

In this respect, the Helsinki declaration is a cause for some concern for the United States, as it continues to stress the need for EU autonomy over the involvement of non–EU states in decision making. Although it argues that "NATO remains the foundation of the collective defense of its members and will continue to have an

Two goals are at odds—EU autonomy vs. letting non–EU states influence decisions

important role in crisis management," this does not imply that NATO will endure as Europe's pivotal security organization. In the future, Europe may well be capable of taking autonomous military action without recourse to NATO and even without first asking the United States to become involved. This is the scenario which Washington fears may provoke a transatlantic decoupling and, thus, spell the end of NATO as we know it—i.e., a NATO based on American supremacy. Although this would not necessarily be a serious disadvantage to Washington, in that a self–reliant EU would take some of the military weight off America's shoulders, the long–term implications could be huge. The EU's combined economic, political, and military influence would transform Europe into a serious rival to the United States on the world stage. EU foreign policy objectives would overlap, but would certainly not be identical to those of the United States. Europeans, for example, remain less fixated on China and on issues of proliferation of weapons of mass destruction (WMD). They are more concerned with legitimizing their policies by international law and a UN Security Council mandate and less hostile to "rogue states" like Iran and Cuba. This implies that a stronger EU would not always have to be in full agreement with the United States on many important global political issues.

Plans for a new Euro-force remain modest and accomplish little more than enabling the EU to take military action without the United States

For the time being, however, the likelihood of autonomous, EU–led military operations is remote. Although path–breaking, the Helsinki summit plans for a new Euro–force remain modest and would accomplish little more than to enable the EU to take military action if the United States does not want to be involved. For many years to come any European–led military operation will remain highly dependent upon NATO command structures as well as on US intelligence and logistics, if not more. It is, therefore, difficult to foresee how the EU would mount any serious operation without at least the consent of the United States. But, it is the continuing uncertainty and vagueness of the operational details of the EU's military structure and its future missions that cause concern across the Atlantic. In an effort to assuage

American concerns, the EU has proposed to offer key NATO military representatives permanent seats, or observer status, in the EU's PSC and MC. Another EU proposal offers NATO's Deputy Supreme Allied Commander Europe (DSACEUR) to participate, "as appropriate," in the EU's MC. In any case, of the 15 EU Member States, 11 plan to send the same representatives to the EU and NATO military committees, which should ensure both transparency and relatively smooth cooperation.

However, the higher mathematics of consultation mechanisms do not inform us what the "New EU" actually plans to do with its fresh military power. This remains unclear. For the time being, Europe's CESDP is bound to have limited, regional ambitions. The EU debate focuses on Petersberg missions and not on territorial or collective defense and, therefore, does not touch upon Article V of WEU's founding treaty (which offers a mutual assistance guarantee). Europe's military strategic planning will, therefore, focus on regional concerns and will not, at least not yet, adopt a global scope. However, whereas London has coined the phrase that the EU will operate "in and around Europe," Mr. Solana is already talking about an EU which might want to act in Africa as well as in East Timor,[16] and German Chancellor Gerhard Schröder has argued that "[t]he Europe of the future must be able to defend its interests and values effectively worldwide."[17] The European Commission's *Strategic Objectives* report of February 2000 also argues that the EU should aim at a "Europe which can show genuine leadership on the world stage."[18]

However, although retaining a regional focus might acquiesce to American demands, it also complicates an already grim transatlantic debate on NATO's role in preventing the proliferation of WMD. In addition to the US Senate's rejection of the comprehensive nuclear test ban treaty, the Clinton administration also wants to tinker with the existing Anti–Ballistic Missile (ABM) Treaty, proposing that the United States set up its own national missile shield. Many European states worry that this will not only set off another global arms race, but may also decouple the strategic interests within the Alliance, when the United States becomes less vulnerable to missile attacks. In any case, this global/regional dichotomy is bound to increase transatlantic tensions and to exacerbate US concern over Europe's defense ambitions.

Some of America's doubt and unease over Europe's new defense initiatives do not spring from political worries concerning NATO's future centrality, but rather are a result of the realization that European countries will buy fewer American weapons in the future. Since the war in Kosovo, the United States has called upon its European allies to spend more on defense, implying that Europe should reequip itself with advanced American technology. The recent series of pan–European defense–industrial mergers has upset American policy makers and analysts, because the EU's CESDP is now likely to be built upon a solid, European defense–industrial base in which the United States only plays a marginal role. Until Autumn 1999, Washington expected that its own defense giants would absorb European firms or set up US–led transatlantic defense groupings. However, since October 1999, the process of European defense consolidation has acquired momentum with the merger of France's Aerospatiale Matra SA and Germany's DaimlerChrysler Aerospace (DASA). The newly–created European Aeronautic Defense and Space Co. (EADS) is bound to seriously rival America's hegemony in the defense–industrial field, although it is still far from reaching commercial and technological parity with the United States.[19]

Europe's drive to consolidate its defense industry comes at a time when American defense companies are exploring their business opportunities in Europe and elsewhere with even more vigor. This is why many in Washington grumble about an emerging "Fortress Europe" and are calling for the revival of a transatlantic concept of defense–industrial cooperation. It is possible that defense alliances on opposite sides of the Atlantic will bitterly compete. The conflict experienced here may well spill over into the political arena and add to the transatlantic strain.[20] But, unless Washington changes its attitude toward the transfer of technology to its NATO allies—technology transfer remains strictly controlled—it is difficult to foresee an expansion of transatlantic defense partnerships.

Russian Reactions, Central European Concerns

Europe's new defense ambitions not only demand a rethinking of NATO's role and the future of the transatlantic relationship, but also have a serious impact on the strategic environment of all Central and East European countries, including Russia. The general trend in Moscow's governmental circles is to welcome the EU's military plans as a step toward ridding Europe of American hegemony and NATO–centrism. From this perspective, a European CESDP is seen as a means to block the creation of a unipolar world led by the United States.[21] Not very surprisingly, this may also be one of the main reasons why many Central European countries are cautious about dealing with defense issues outside the well–known and tested NATO framework. Countries like the Czech Republic, Hungary, and Poland fear that Europe's defense plans may undermine the relevance of NATO—and its Article V collective defense guarantee in particular. These new NATO allies are also not assured that the United States will draw the right conclusions from these recent EU initiatives.

They understand that the United States might, on the contrary, decide to leave the management of European security to the Europeans themselves.

Since most Central European countries lack institutional ties to the EU to make a serious impact on the CESDP, this next section will mainly address the fundamental reasons for Central Europe's concerns regarding recent developments. Moscow's more positive reactions also merit discussion, because Russia's strategic weight in Europe's security framework remains considerable.

Moscow's Perspective on European Defense. Most Russian official statements and publications on West European defense and politico–military cooperation are set in a positive tone, quite unlike the Russian debate over NATO and its enlargement process. In–depth knowledge and analysis of the Byzantine workings of the EU and its activities are, however, rare and limited to a small circle of experts and specialists. The general public in Russia has practically no knowledge of the EU and WEU. This also implies that—again, unlike NATO— the EU/WEU are not perceived as an antagonistic military bloc. Even though WEU offers a mutual military commitment quite similar to that of NATO, it did not acquire an inimical image in the USSR and was never perceived as a primary instrument of western policy toward communism. It is indeed significant that, contrary to what has happened with NATO, the intensive development of WEU's military dimension and its process of enlargement have not provoked a negative reaction in Russia. When WEU decided in May 1994 to offer Central European countries (including the three Baltic states) the status of Associate Partner, Russian Foreign Minister Andrei Kozyrev stated that Russia had no objections to this move. Quite to the contrary, European initiatives to strengthen the political independence and military capabilities of WEU have generally met with tacit or explicit Russian approval. For example, when the North Atlantic Council endorsed, at the Berlin ministerial meeting in June 1996, the concept of WEU using NATO assets for WEU–led operations, Russian Minister of Defense Pavel Grachev officially welcomed "the increased role of WEU in solving West European problems," and noted that the "increased independence of WEU from NATO" should be considered a "very positive fact."[22]

During the Cold War, it was widely assumed that the USSR actively encouraged West European military cooperation in an effort to weaken the transatlantic link and to "decouple" the United States from its European allies. Although there was certainly an element of *divide et impere* in the Soviet approach to the institutional management of European security, this should, nevertheless, be considered to have been a minor ingredient in an overwhelmingly Atlanticist policy based on the assumption that the United States dominated NATO and its decision making. The Russians may have tried to encourage Europe to assume more autonomy in the military field, but during the Cold War they realized that European room for maneuver was very limited.

A decade after the fall of the Berlin Wall this has all changed, and Russia now has a heightened interest in the EU/WEU and the European integration process.[23] The EU and Russia signed a Partnership and Cooperation Agreement (PCA) in June 1994 which, apart from dealing with trade issues, institutionalizes a broad political dialogue between two "partners." The EU has placed Russia in a pivotal position in the debate on European security and has emphasized the fact that the EU is interested in the "full involvement of Russia in the development of a comprehensive European security

**Russia is prepared
to be positive
about the EU's
defense plans**

architecture in which Russia has its
due place."[24]   Although Moscow
does not yet take the EU/WEU too
seriously as a partner in the area of
security and defense, Russia realizes
that   Europe's   new   military
ambitions have a broader and more
comprehensive character than the classic defense alliance of
NATO. It appears that Russia is prepared to adopt a more
unbiased and even positive approach to the EU's defense
plans, especially in comparison to Moscow's unveiled hostility
vis–à–vis NATO enlargement.

Related to this issue is the fact that the EU is now Russia's
main trading partner (with whom Russia had an export surplus
of almost 10 billion euro in 1999), its main investor, as well as
its largest donor of assistance and grants (under the so–called
Technical Assistance to the Commonwealth of Independent
States [TACIS] program). The PCA formalizes the
EU–Russian relationship and includes a security dimension.
The EU adopted its Common Strategy on Russia at the
Cologne summit of June 1999. The Common Strategy has
done much to consolidate and galvanize a more general and
comprehensive EU approach toward Russia. Although WEU
regards developments in Russia to be a vital security interest,
it has been reluctant to institutionalize its relationship with
Moscow. Russia and WEU, however, do engage in a number
of practical cooperative projects. In November 1995, for
example, a commercial contract was signed between the WEU
Satellite Centre in Torrejón, Spain, and the Russian state
armaments company *Rosvoorouzhenie*.[25]   Since 1997, WEU
and Moscow have also been discussing the possibilities of
making Russian long–haul air transport assets available to
WEU for certain Petersberg missions.[26]   In addition, in terms

of building political contacts, the relationship is clearly moving into a higher gear, without yet becoming institutionalized.

In their analysis of the Russian approach toward WEU, Dmitryi Danilov and Stephan De Spiegeleire note a number of other reasons why Russia seems to be comfortable with the EU's defense plans. First, West European military–political cooperation and integration do not pose a direct threat to Russian security as long as WEU's collective defense functions have *de facto* been delegated to NATO. Second, the EU's and WEU's focus on Petersberg missions seems to create a benign psychological climate in Russia which makes cooperation with the EU/WEU easier and politically less sensitive. Third, Europe's efforts to set up a CESDP clearly point in the direction of a strengthening and *rapprochement* of Western Europe's security institutions (WEU and the EU's CFSP), which will inevitably increase Europe's roles and responsibilities. These developments are perceived positively within Russia, mainly because they strengthen Western Europe's voice within NATO, which may give Russia more political incentives and possibilities for cooperation with the Alliance. All in all, Danilov and De Spiegeleire argue, a stronger institutional embodiment of the European Security and Defense Identity (ESDI) will contribute to the establishment of a new "triangle" around which a European security equilibrium will be structured: the United States/Western Europe/Russia.

Clearly the "weakest chain" in this emerging security triangle is the relatively underdeveloped link between the EU/WEU and Russia. Following the EU's Common Strategy on Russia of 1999, Moscow has worked out its own official policy *vis–à–vis* the EU and the European integration process in general. This document, called *Medium–Term Strategy for Development of Relations Between the Russian Federation and the European Union*, was officially approved by the Russian government in October 1999. The strategy starts by claiming that Russia's aim is to make use of the EU's economic potential and managerial experience in order to assist Russia's goals of achieving a socially oriented market economy and a law–ruled democratic state. For the first time, Moscow acknowledges that it is not in its interest to join the EU as a full member. The strategy then proceeds to call for cooperation with the EU to "ensure pan–European security by the Europeans themselves without both isolation of the United States and NATO and their dominance on the continent." The strategy also envisions "practical cooperation [between Russia and the EU] in the area of security (peacemaking, crisis management, various aspects of arms limitation and reduction, etc.) which could counterbalance, *inter alia*, the NATO–centrism in Europe." It is telling that of the 20–page document, a mere single paragraph is devoted to the security aspects of EU–Russian cooperation; the remainder is devoted to trade, financial cooperation, the impact of EU enlargement, etc.

This may again illustrate that, for the time being, the EU's defense ambitions do not register prominently on the strategic radar screen of policy makers and analysts in Moscow. However, given the scheduled enlargement of the EU, Russia will no doubt come to see the "New EU" not only as a mainly economic partner, but also as a possible challenger to Russia's traditional sphere of interest in Central Europe. EU enlargement is likely to include the Baltic states as well as most other former Warsaw Pact countries. If not managed properly, this will no doubt add to the traditional Russian trauma of isolation and seclusion from the core of Europe.

Most likely, Russia will only really take serious notice of the EU's increasing defense capabilities when confronted with them during a crisis or conflict. When EU–led peacekeeping troops start to operate closer to Russia's traditional sphere of interest, Moscow may easily change its mind on the assumed positive aspects of Europe's defense consolidation. At the same time, a complete reversal of Moscow's current constructive attitude is equally unlikely, because its economic and trade ties with the EU region are too valuable for Russia to forgo.

Central Europe's Fear of Decoupling. It used to be rather straightforward: NATO was in the business of "hard security," dealing with defense issues, whereas the EU took care of economics and trade, preparing the groundwork for political and cultural cooperation and dealing with other "soft security" matters. WEU essentially remained, at most, a sleeping beauty that nobody wanted—or dared—to kiss awake. Given the decisions made at the EU's Helsinki summit, this seemingly clear–cut division of labor has become a thing of the past.

Of course, such a tidy division of tasks never really existed, and the European integration process has always had marked political and security implications. But, particularly for Central European countries, this institutional order was attractive because it firmly embedded the United States in all

Few Central European countries want the EU to take more responsibility for defense

important security calculations in Europe, especially those of a military nature. What is more, because NATO has proven to be easier to join than the EU, Central European countries do not, in general, look forward to a new division of tasks where the

EU takes more responsibility for defense matters. Contrary to their counterparts in Western Europe, Central European policy makers and analysts tend to emphasize the continued importance of a credible and robust collective defense commitment (*à la* NATO's Article 5). For many Central Europeans it is only the defense commitment of NATO, and of the United States in particular, that offers them a credible security guarantee. Because the EU lacks military clout and practical experience, it is not considered the organization of choice to handle defense issues. For the time being, the EU's defense ambitions do not exceed Petersberg missions and exclude territorial defense (which remain entrusted to NATO). But, Central Europeans seem more concerned than anyone else that this may only be the beginning of a long and uncertain process of transferring more and more defense tasks from NATO to the EU. Were this to occur, the management of European security would become only tangentially linked to NATO, and this would result in the dreaded scenario of a decoupling of the United States from Europe.

However, for the moment, Central Europe's greatest concern is that major decisions concerning Europe's defense policy are made by current EU Member States.[27] Although most Central European countries are engaged in accession negotiations and have established multiple channels for consultation and the exchange of ideas and information (most notably through European agreements and the EU's reinforced pre–accession strategy *vis–à–vis* Central Europe), they are not really involved in the debate over the shape of European defense within the EU. The Helsinki *communiqué* argues that it is the EU's responsibility to ensure that the "necessary dialogue" concerning the EU's new defense role takes place with EU accession candidates. The *communiqué* fails, however, to specify how the dialogue is to take place and whether it is to go beyond consultation. Hungary's President Arpad Goencz argued in January 2000 that his country, "as an associate member of the Western European Union, intends to take an active part in the formulation of the European security and defense identity."[28] However, Goencz's statement glosses over the fact that Hungary (as all other Central European countries) is not a member of the EU yet, which makes all the difference. Polish diplomats have expressed their concern, noting that by establishing a politico–military committee within the EU, Europe is *de facto* mimicking NATO's North Atlantic Council and Military Committee, thereby strengthening the EU's "natural tendencies" for independent military action without full agreement of the United States.[29] For Central European countries this is an especially sensitive point, because the general feeling is that, as Poland's Foreign Affairs Minister Bronislaw Geremek argued, "[e]xperience of history indicates that it is better when the United States are engaged in European affairs."[30]

As Associate Members of WEU, the Czech Republic, Hungary, and Poland call upon the EU to maintain their current close involvement in the development of the ESDI. WEU Associate Members (i.e., those European NATO members that are not EU Member States),[31] are fully engaged in the discussions within WEU and can fully participate in its activities and military operations. These Central European countries, therefore, highlight the importance of transferring the rights they enjoy as WEU Associate Members to the new structures to be developed inside the EU. This, they argue, would allow them to participate fully in the possible formulation of the EU's defense convergence criteria as well as in the preparation and execution of the EU's future military operations. Most importantly, however, it would assure that they have a voice in the decision shaping process within the

EU. This would allow them to be involved in substantive, day–to–day consultations on issues related to Europe's military future and to participate in shaping the organizational structure of the complex EU–WEU–NATO relationship. It would also provide them with assured equal rights with EU members in future EU–led military operations.

Hungary's Prime Minister Viktor Orban has, therefore, called upon his Central European colleagues to coordinate their approach to the EU's defense plans, because "[t]hese are not the exclusive issues of Western European states; these are Central European questions as well. We are aware of a Slovak, a Hungarian, a Polish, and a Czech position on this question, but we have never coordinated our positions on these strategic issues and we have no real joint Central European strategic planning."[32] A coordinated position will be all the more necessary since the three front running EU candidates (the Czech Republic, Poland, and Hungary) are expected to join the EU sometime between 2003 and 2007. This is also the time frame for the establishment of the Euro–force, to which the current applicant countries are likely to make military contributions. It remains uncertain as to whether countries like Bulgaria and Romania will join the EU or NATO first, or how they could contribute to EU–led military operations. The three Baltic countries are in a strategically delicate position as former Soviet republics, in that Russia's firm opposition to their NATO membership may well extend to the preclusion of any future Baltic participation in the EU's military structures. Moscow has always been moderately positive in regard to Baltic plans to join the EU. However, it is hard to predict whether Russia will adopt a more hostile attitude toward the Baltic when the Baltic states join the EU, once a more robust and vigorous European CESDP manifests itself.

In Conclusion

Helsinki testifies to a sea change in attitudes among Europeans on the still sensitive issue of a common European defense policy. One should not forget that a decade ago the debate over Europe's single currency was about "whether" it could ever become reality, whereas in 2000, we are talking about "how" to make it a success. A similar shift from "whether" to "how" has occurred in the debate on European defense, now that "Kosovo" has broken down many old shibboleths against joint Europe–led military operations. In addition to political reasons, defense cooperation is driven by the potential to eliminate costly redundancies among European armed forces. All this implies that many European states are willing to pool the core of their national sovereignty and are prepared to take one more step toward a qualitatively new Euro–polity.[33]

No doubt, this will take getting used to by Americans and Europeans alike. It will also require a change of mind and intellectual flexibility on the parts of Russia and Central European countries in their approach to the future organization of European security. Although the transatlantic relationship may have reached another of its (in)famous "crossroads," there is no reason to assume the dawn of an era of "transatlantic troubles." Washington tends to support European cooperation as long as it takes weight off American shoulders, but not if it challenges America's own political primacy and economic interests. On its part, Europe will have to get used to thinking about *European*, instead of narrow national interests which may well have to be defended with *European* military means. The last time British troops fought under a German operational command was in 1813, at the Battle of Leipzig. Yet, in October 1999, General Klaus Reinhardt of Germany took over as commander of the Kosovo peacekeeping force, and overall command of KFOR was taken by the Eurocorps in April 2000.[34] All European countries will have to get used to these historic novelties. There is little doubt that European countries have sufficient military experience and leadership qualities to take on these challenges. However, like the EMU and the euro, much will depend upon the willingness of Europeans to trust their own strength and capabilities. Will Europeans, and others, be prepared to put their faith in an organization that has brought them such bureaucratic nightmares as the Common Agricultural Policy (CAP), and which is tarnished by a reputation for sluggish and ineffectual decision making (albeit not really justified)?

Just dial 00-32-2-285-500-00 to reach the EU's new situation and crisis center

In the event of a serious crisis, "Europe" finally has a relevant telephone number, which many Americans have called for; just dial 00–32–2–285–500–00 and one will reach the EU's new situation and crisis center, headed by Solana. Whether this will improve the quality of the transatlantic dialogue remains to be seen. For the time being, the underlying forces within NATO are more competitive than cooperative. Because the scope and form of Europe's CESDP will remain undecided for quite some time, the United States should have ample opportunity to affect the shape of a more balanced transatlantic relationship in which NATO will no longer play the central role. Anyone who expects that the strategic arrangement of NATO, shaped by the Cold War, could remain frozen a decade beyond its thaw is not a realist. Without a rebalanced transatlantic relationship, NATO will certainly fall into decay. On the other hand, if Europe's CESDP is injudiciously managed, Europe may end up with the worst of both worlds: a weak EU and a weakened NATO.[35] One thing is therefore certain: If Europeans continue to depend upon the United States for their long–term military security, NATO will not survive, at least not as the pivotal point for European defense. ∎

Endnotes

1. A shorter version of this paper was published as "Europe's Common Defense Policy: Implications for the Trans Atlantic Relationship," *Security Dialogue*, Vol. 31, No. 2, June 2000, pp. 219–232.
2. *Financial Times*, September 15, 1999.
3. Margarita Mathiopoulos and Istvan Gyarmati, "Saint Malo and Beyond: Toward European Defense," *The Washington Quarterly*, Vol. 22, No. 4, Autumn 1999, pp. 65–76.
4. British Prime Minister Tony Blair, "NATO, Europe, and Our Future Security," speech at the NATO 50th Anniversary conference, Royal United Services Institute, London, March 8, 1999.
5. Paul J. Teunissen, "Strengthening the Defence Dimension of the EU: An Evaluation of Concepts, Recent Initiatives and Development," *European Foreign Affairs Review*, Vol. 4, No. 3, Autumn 1999, pp. 327–352.
6. Ian Kemp, "Pressure for EU Rapid Reaction Force Gains New Momentum," *Jane's Defence Weekly*, December 1, 1999.
7. US Deputy Secretary of State Strobe Talbott, speech to the North Atlantic Council, Brussels, December 15, 1999.
8. For a few exceptions see Charles A. Kupchan, "Life After Pax Americana," *World Policy Journal*, Vol. 16, No. 3, Fall 1999, pp. 20–27; Benjamin Schwarz and Christopher Layne, "NATO: At 50, It's Time to Quit," *The Nation*, May 10, 1999, pp. 15–19; and Stephen M. Walt, "The Ties That Fray: Why Europe and America are Drifting Apart," *The National Interest*, No. 54, Winter 1998/99, pp. 3–11.
9. *International Herald Tribune*, March 6, 2000.
10. Quoted in the *New York Times*, December 13, 1999.
11. Quoted in *Defense Daily*, December 8, 1999.
12. Quoted in the *Financial Times*, October 22, 1999.
13. Quoted in the *New York Times*, December 2, 1999.
14. Mathias Jopp, *European Defence Policy: The Debate on the Institutional Aspects*, Bonn: Institut für Europäische Politik, June/July 1999, pp. 26–29. See also Alyson Bailes, "European Defence: What Are the 'Convergence Criteria'?" *RUSI Journal*, Vol. 144, No. 3, June 1999, pp. 60–65.

15. Quoted in *The Times*, November 23, 1999.

16. Siegesmund von Ilsemann, Dirk Koch, and Alexander Szandar, "Europa Baut eigene Armee" ("Europe Builds Its Own Army"), *Der Spiegel*, November 29, 1999, pp.188–91.

17. Quoted in the *New York Times*, December 13, 1999.

18. Commission of the European Communities, "Strategic Objectives 2000–2005—Shaping the New Europe," Brussels, February 9, 2000, p. 4.

19. The Spanish Construcciones Aeronáuticas S. A. (CASA) aerospace group joined the EADS in December 1999. EADS now controls 80 per cent of the Airbus consortium, 43 per cent of Eurofighter and has almost all of Europe's military transport aircraft, missiles, spacecraft, and helicopters within its portfolio. See Paul Baever, "European Giant is Born," *Jane's Defence Weekly*, December 8, 1999.

20. For a balanced American view, see John Deutsch, Arnold Kanter, and Brent Scowcroft, "Saving NATO's Foundation," *Foreign Affairs*, Vol. 78, No. 6, November/December 1999, pp. 54–67.

21. *Medium–Term Strategy for Development of Relations Between the Russian Federation and the European Union*, Moscow: October 1999, para. 1.5.2.

22. Quoted in Dmitriy Danilov and Stephan De Spiegeleire, *From Decoupling to Recoupling. Russia and Western Europe: A New Security Relationship*, Chaillot Paper No. 31, Paris: WEU–ISS, April 1998, p. 7.

23. For a few historical notes, see John Roper and Peter van Ham, "Russia and the West," in Vladimir Baranovski, ed., *Russia in Europe: The Emerging Security Agenda*, London/Oxford: Oxford University Press, 1997; and Heinz Timmerman, "Relations Between the EU and Russia: The Agreement on Partnership and Co–operation," *Journal of Communist Studies and Transition Politics*, Vol. 12, No. 2, June 1996, pp. 196–223.

24. This declaration was made by the EU during the "Security Working Group" troika–meetings with Russia on October 10, 1996, preparing the OSCE's "Security Model for the Twenty–First Century." For a good overview and analysis of the EU's policy toward Russia, see Marie–Elisabeth de Vel and Hannes Adomeit, "The European Union's Long–Term Strategy Towards Russia," CPN Briefing Paper from the Stiftung Wissenschaft und Politik, February 2000.

25. Richard Tibbels, "WEU's Dialogues With Russia and Ukraine," *NATO's Sixteen Nations & Partners for Peace*, February 1998, pp. 43–46.

26. It is worth noting that WEU has agreed on similar arrangements with Ukraine. In June 1999, WEU stated in a press release that "[t]he areas of practical cooperation relate primarily to the preparation for crisis management operations and include Ukraine's observation of exercises at WEU, the availability to WEU nations of Ukrainian training facilities as well as the fields of long–haul transport and satellite imagery."

[27.] *Süddeutsche Zeitung*, February 23, 2000.

[28.] *BBC Monitoring European–Political*, January 17, 2000.

[29.] *Rzeczpospolita*, Warsaw, December 20, 1999.

[30.] *Rzeczpospolita*, Warsaw, December 16, 1999.

[31.] Only Denmark does not fit this description. Denmark is only involved in WEU as an Observer, but is, of course, also a full member of NATO and the EU.

[32.] *BBC Monitoring European–Political*, August 30, 1999.

[33.] Peter van Ham and Przemyslaw Grudzinski, "Affluence and Influence: The Conceptual Basis of Europe's New Politics," *The National Interest*, No. 58, Winter 1999/2000, pp. 81–87.

[34.] The suggestion to take this step was made by France and Germany on December 2, 1999.

[35.] For a general discussion of the problem of rising expectations and moderate adaptations of capabilities see: Christopher Hill, "The Capability–Expectations Gap, or Conceptualizing Europe's International Role," *Journal of Common Market Studies*, Vol. 31, No. 3, September 1993, pp. 305–328.

Acronyms

ABM - Anti-Ballistic Missile
CDP - Common Defence Policy (EU)
CESDP - Common European Security and Defence Policy (EU)
CFSP - Common Foreign and Security Policy (EU)
CAP - Common Agricultural Policy (EU)
DASA - DaimlerChrysler Aerospace
EADS - European Aeronautic Defense and Space Co.
EDC - European Defence Community (EU)
EMU - European Monetary Union
ESDI - European Security and Defense Identity (EU)
EU - European Union
MC - Military Committee (EU)
MS - Military Staff (EU)
NAC - North Atlantic Council (NATO)
NATO - North Atlantic Treaty Organization
PCA - Partnership and Cooperation Agreement (EU-Russia)
PSC - Political and Security Committee (EU)
TACIS - Technical Assistance to the Commonwealth of Independent
　　　　　States (EU)
WEU - Western European Union
WMD - Weapons of Mass Destruction

The George C. Marshall
European Center for Security Studies

Dr. Robert Kennedy
Director

MG (Ret.) Franz Werner
German Deputy Director

Ambassador Victor Jackovich
Associate Director for International Affairs

College of International and Security Studies

Dr. Gary L. Guertner
Dean

Dr. Peter van Ham (Author)
Professor of West European Politics

Ms. Sara C. Holman
Editor

Mr. Michael J. McNulty
Distribution